NBA CHAMPIONS LOS ANGELES LAKERS

AARON FRISCH

CREATIVE EDUCATION

Published by Creative Education
P.O. Box 227, Mankato, Minnesota 56002
Creative Education is an imprint of The Creative Company
www.thecreativecompany.us

Book and cover design by Blue Design (www.bluedes.com)
Art direction by Rita Marshall
Printed by Corporate Graphics in the United States of
America

Photographs by Basketballphoto.com (Steve Lipofsky),
Corbis (Jeff Lewis/Icon SMI), Getty Images (Andrew D.
Bernstein/NBAE, Walter Bibikow, James Drake/Sports
Illustrated, Noah Graham/NBAE, Wendi Kaminski/NBAE,
George Long/Sports Illustrated, NBAP/NBAE, NBAE Photos/
NBAE, Mike Powell/Allsport), US Presswire (Manny Rubio)

Library of Congress Cataloging-in-Publication Data

Frisch, Aaron.
Los Angeles Lakers / by Aaron Frisch.
p. cm. — (NBA champions)
Includes bibliographical references and index.
Summary: A basic introduction to the Los Angeles Lakers
professional basketball team, including its formation
in Minneapolis, Minnesota, in 1947, greatest players,
championships, and stars of today.
ISBN 978-1-60818-136-0
1. Los Angeles Lakers (Basketball team)—History—Juvenile
literature. I. Title.
GV885.52.L67F75 2011
796.323'640979494—dc22   2010051211

CPSIA: 030111 PO1448

First edition
9 8 7 6 5 4 3 2 1

Cover: Kobe Bryant
Page 2: Pau Gasol
Right: Jerry West
Page 6: Wilt Chamberlain

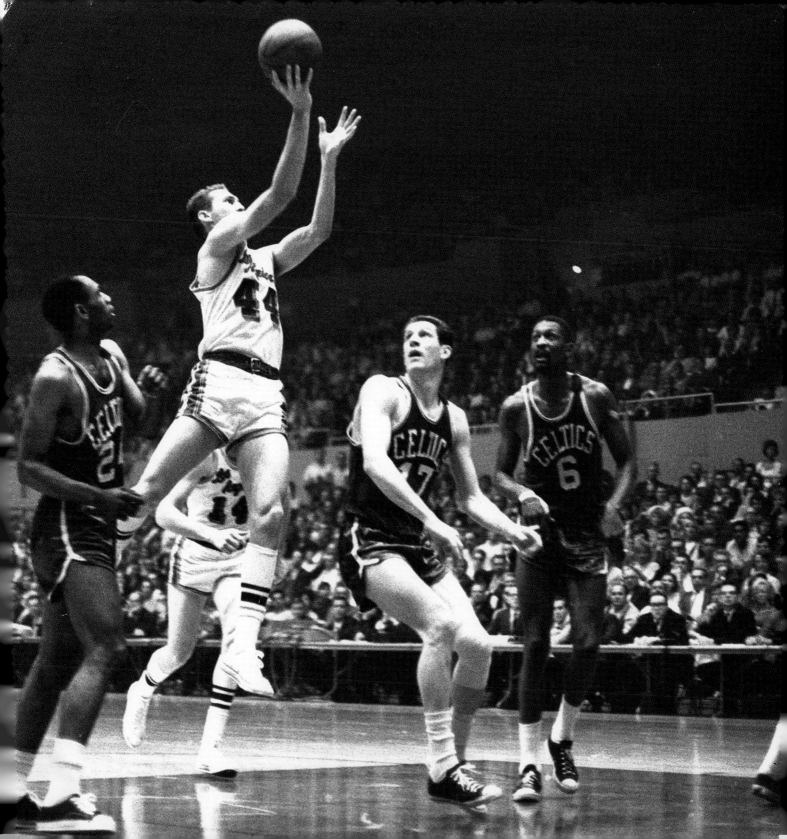

TABLE OF CONTENTS

People sometimes call Los Angeles "L.A." for short

Los Angeles is a city in California. Los Angeles is a huge, sunny city on the west coast of the United States. It has an **arena** called Staples Center that is the home of a basketball team called the Lakers.

Staples Center has seats for more than 19,000 basketball fans

The Lakers are part of the National Basketball Association (NBA). All the teams in the NBA try to win the NBA Finals to become world champions. The Lakers play many games against teams called the Clippers, Kings, Suns, and Warriors.

The Lakers started playing in 1947. They played in Minneapolis, Minnesota, then. The Lakers were a great team right away. They were world champions five times in six seasons!

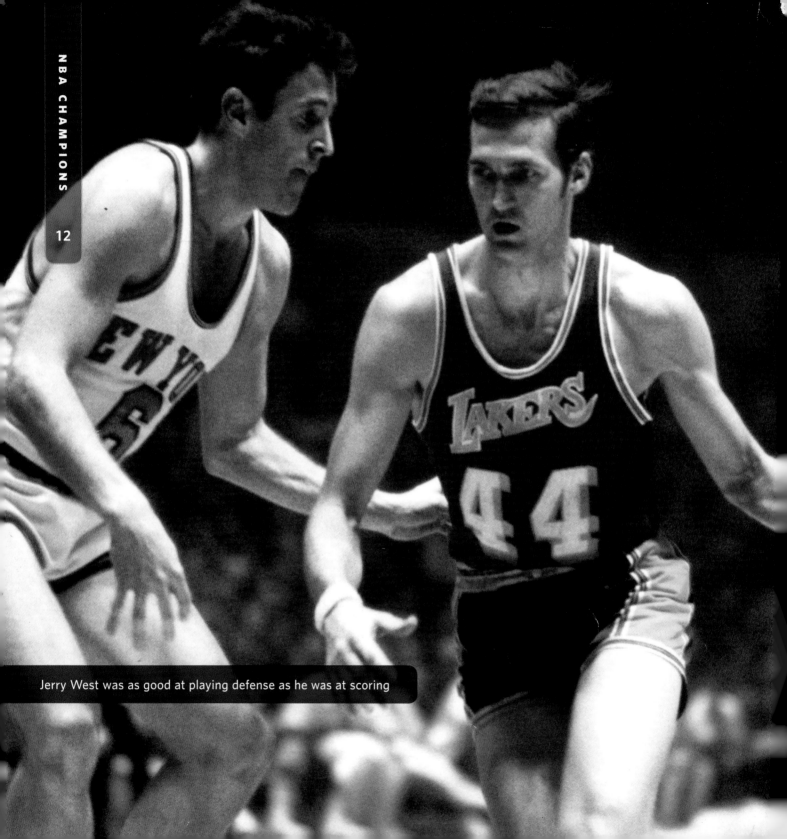

Jerry West was as good at playing defense as he was at scoring

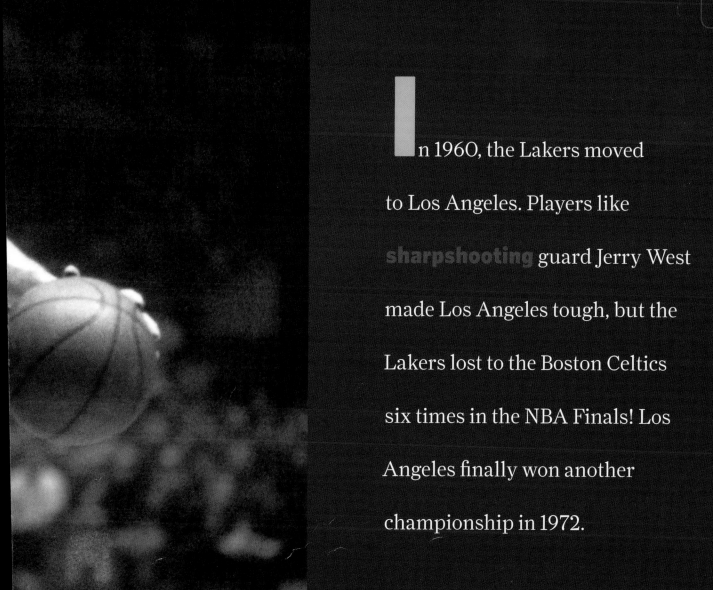

Why Are They Called the Lakers?

The Lakers started out in Minnesota. There are a lot of lakes there. There are so many lakes that Minnesota is nicknamed "The Land of 10,000 Lakes"!

In 1960, the Lakers moved to Los Angeles. Players like sharpshooting guard Jerry West made Los Angeles tough, but the Lakers lost to the Boston Celtics six times in the NBA Finals! Los Angeles finally won another championship in 1972.

LAKERS FACTS

- Started playing: 1947

- Conference/division: Western Conference, Pacific Division

- Team colors: gold and purple

- NBA championships:

  1949 — 4 games to 2 versus Washington Capitols

  1950 — 4 games to 2 versus Syracuse Nationals

  1952 — 4 games to 3 versus New York Knicks

  1953 — 4 games to 1 versus New York Knicks

  1954 — 4 games to 3 versus Syracuse Nationals

  1972 — 4 games to 1 versus New York Knicks

  1980 — 4 games to 2 versus Philadelphia 76ers

  1982 — 4 games to 2 versus Philadelphia 76ers

  1985 — 4 games to 2 versus Boston Celtics

  1987 — 4 games to 2 versus Boston Celtics

  1988 — 4 games to 3 versus Detroit Pistons

  2000 — 4 games to 2 versus Indiana Pacers

  2001 — 4 games to 1 versus Philadelphia 76ers

  2002 — 4 games to 0 versus New Jersey Nets

  2009 — 4 games to 1 versus Orlando Magic

  2010 — 4 games to 3 versus Boston Celtics

- NBA Web site for kids: http://www.nba.com/kids/

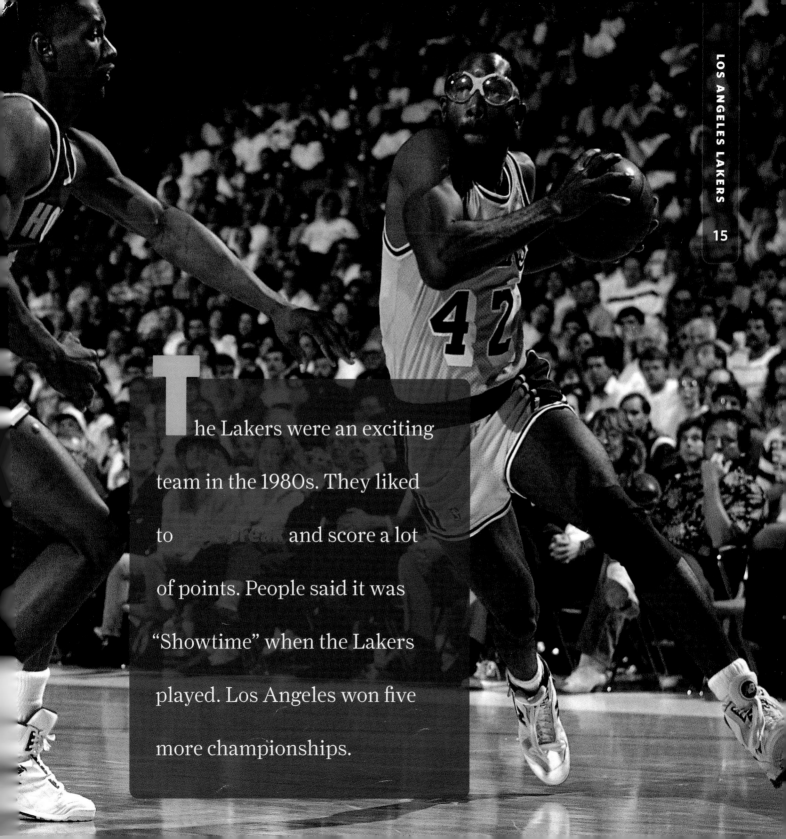

The Lakers were an exciting team in the 1980s. They liked to fastbreak and score a lot of points. People said it was "Showtime" when the Lakers played. Los Angeles won five more championships.

Huge center Shaquille O'Neal and smart coach Phil Jackson joined the Lakers after that, and Los Angeles kept winning. The Lakers were NBA champs in 2000, 2001, and 2002. In 2010, they won their 16th NBA **title**!

SAY IT LIKE THIS

Shaquille
shuh-KEEL

Shaquille O'Neal was probably the strongest player in the NBA

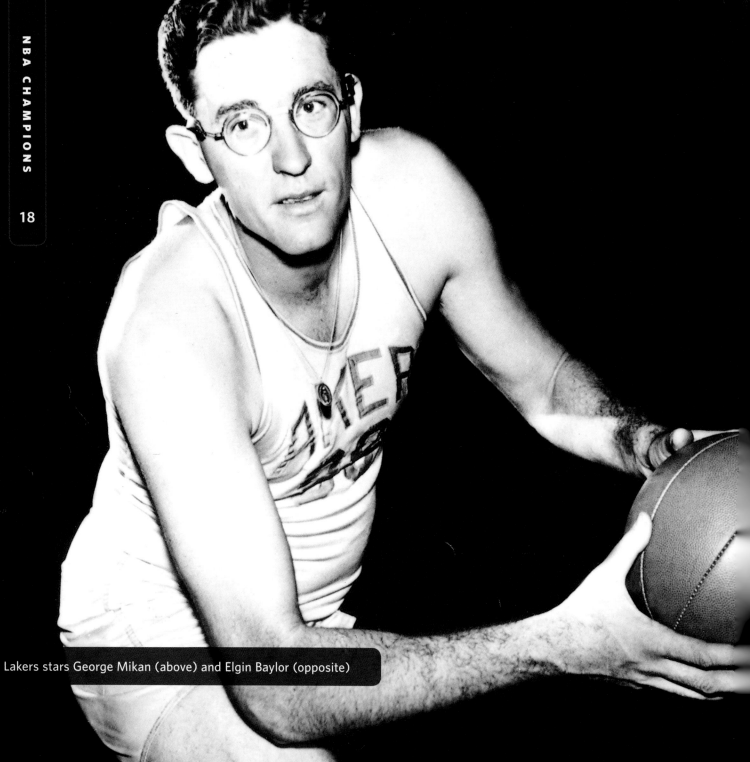

Lakers stars George Mikan (above) and Elgin Baylor (opposite)

T wo of the Lakers' first stars were center George Mikan and forward Elgin Baylor. Mikan was the best **big man** in the early days of the NBA. Baylor was a great scorer who excited fans with his high-jumping shots.

SAY IT LIKE THIS

Mikan
MY-ken

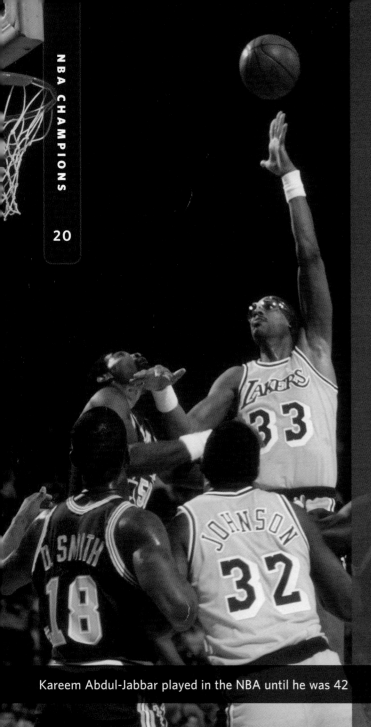

Kareem Abdul-Jabbar played in the NBA until he was 42

Center Kareem Abdul-Jabbar joined Los Angeles in 1975. He scored more points than any other player in NBA history. Tall guard Magic Johnson was another Lakers star. He was famous for his fancy passes.

SAY IT LIKE THIS

Kareem
Abdul-Jabbar
*kuh-REEM ab-DOOL
juh-BAR*

Star Magic Johnson led the Lakers to five NBA championships

The Lakers added guard Kobe Bryant in 1996. He won an award as the NBA's best player in 2008. Los Angeles fans hoped that he would help lead the Lakers to their 17th NBA championship!

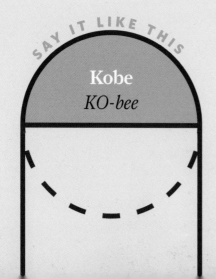

SAY IT LIKE THIS

Kobe
KO-bee

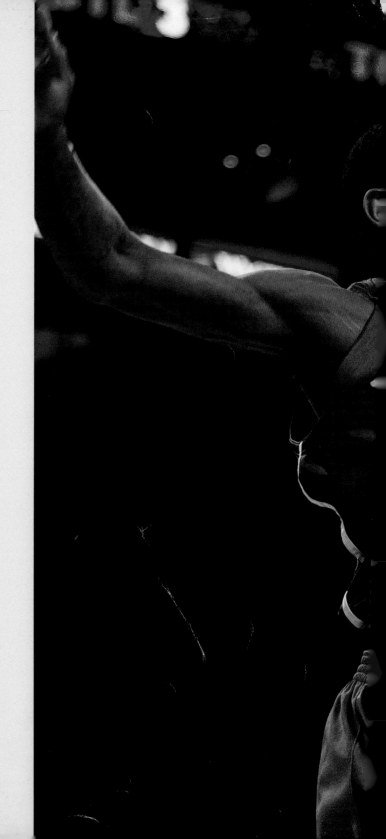

Kobe Bryant could jump high and make many exciting shots

GLOSSARY

arena — a large building for indoor sports events; it has many seats for fans

big man — a basketball player who plays as a forward or center

fast-break — to run down the basketball court and try to score a basket quickly

NBA Finals — a series of games between two teams at the end of the playoffs; the first team to win four games is the champion

sharpshooting — good at making shots from a long distance

title — another word for championship

INDEX